THIS BELONGS TO:

Week of

Monday
1
2
3

Tuesday
1
2
3

Wednesday
1
2
3

Thursday
1
2
3

Friday
1
2
3

Saturday
1
2
3

Sunday
1
2
3

Week of

Monday
1
2
3

Tuesday
1
2
3

Wednesday
1
2
3

Thursday
1
2
3

Friday
1
2
3

Saturday
1
2
3

Sunday
1
2
3

WEEK OF

MONDAY
1
2
3

TUESDAY
1
2
3

WEDNESDAY
1
2
3

THURSDAY
1
2
3

FRIDAY
1
2
3

SATURDAY
1
2
3

SUNDAY
1
2
3

Week of

Monday
1
2
3

Tuesday
1
2
3

Wednesday
1
2
3

Thursday
1
2
3

Friday
1
2
3

Saturday
1
2
3

Sunday
1
2
3

Week of

Monday
1
2
3

Tuesday
1
2
3

Wednesday
1
2
3

Thursday
1
2
3

Friday
1
2
3

Saturday
1
2
3

Sunday
1
2
3

Week of

Monday

1

2

3

Tuesday

1

2

3

Wednesday

1

2

3

Thursday

1

2

3

Friday

1

2

3

Saturday

1

2

3

Sunday

1

2

3

Week of

Monday
1
2
3

Tuesday
1
2
3

Wednesday
1
2
3

Thursday
1
2
3

Friday
1
2
3

Saturday
1
2
3

Sunday
1
2
3

Week of

Monday
1
2
3

Tuesday
1
2
3

Wednesday
1
2
3

Thursday
1
2
3

Friday
1
2
3

Saturday
1
2
3

Sunday
1
2
3

WEEK OF

MONDAY
1
2
3

TUESDAY
1
2
3

WEDNESDAY
1
2
3

THURSDAY
1
2
3

FRIDAY
1
2
3

SATURDAY
1
2
3

SUNDAY
1
2
3

Week of

Monday
1
2
3

Tuesday
1
2
3

Wednesday
1
2
3

Thursday
1
2
3

Friday
1
2
3

Saturday
1
2
3

Sunday
1
2
3

Week of

Monday
1
2
3

Tuesday
1
2
3

Wednesday
1
2
3

Thursday
1
2
3

Friday
1
2
3

Saturday
1
2
3

Sunday
1
2
3

WEEK OF

MONDAY
1
2
3

TUESDAY
1
2
3

WEDNESDAY
1
2
3

THURSDAY
1
2
3

FRIDAY
1
2
3

SATURDAY
1
2
3

SUNDAY
1
2
3

Week of

Monday
1
2
3

Tuesday
1
2
3

Wednesday
1
2
3

Thursday
1
2
3

Friday
1
2
3

Saturday
1
2
3

Sunday
1
2
3

Week of

Monday
1
2
3

Tuesday
1
2
3

Wednesday
1
2
3

Thursday
1
2
3

Friday
1
2
3

Saturday
1
2
3

Sunday
1
2
3

Week of

Monday
1
2
3

Tuesday
1
2
3

Wednesday
1
2
3

Thursday
1
2
3

Friday
1
2
3

Saturday
1
2
3

Sunday
1
2
3

Week of

Monday
1
2
3

Tuesday
1
2
3

Wednesday
1
2
3

Thursday
1
2
3

Friday
1
2
3

Saturday
1
2
3

Sunday
1
2
3

Week of

Monday
1
2
3

Tuesday
1
2
3

Wednesday
1
2
3

Thursday
1
2
3

Friday
1
2
3

Saturday
1
2
3

Sunday
1
2
3

Week of

Monday
1
2
3

Tuesday
1
2
3

Wednesday
1
2
3

Thursday
1
2
3

Friday
1
2
3

Saturday
1
2
3

Sunday
1
2
3

Week of

Monday
1
2
3

Tuesday
1
2
3

Wednesday
1
2
3

Thursday
1
2
3

Friday
1
2
3

Saturday
1
2
3

Sunday
1
2
3

Week of

Monday
1
2
3

Tuesday
1
2
3

Wednesday
1
2
3

Thursday
1
2
3

Friday
1
2
3

Saturday
1
2
3

Sunday
1
2
3

Week of

Monday
1
2
3

Tuesday
1
2
3

Wednesday
1
2
3

Thursday
1
2
3

Friday
1
2
3

Saturday
1
2
3

Sunday
1
2
3

Week of

Monday
1
2
3

Tuesday
1
2
3

Wednesday
1
2
3

Thursday
1
2
3

Friday
1
2
3

Saturday
1
2
3

Sunday
1
2
3

Week of

Monday

1
2
3

Tuesday

1
2
3

Wednesday

1
2
3

Thursday

1
2
3

Friday

1
2
3

Saturday

1
2
3

Sunday

1
2
3

Week of

Monday

1

2

3

Tuesday

1

2

3

Wednesday

1

2

3

Thursday

1

2

3

Friday

1

2

3

Saturday

1

2

3

Sunday

1

2

3

Week of

Monday
1
2
3

Tuesday
1
2
3

Wednesday
1
2
3

Thursday
1
2
3

Friday
1
2
3

Saturday
1
2
3

Sunday
1
2
3

WEEK OF

MONDAY
1
2
3

TUESDAY
1
2
3

WEDNESDAY
1
2
3

THURSDAY
1
2
3

FRIDAY
1
2
3

SATURDAY
1
2
3

SUNDAY
1
2
3

Week of

Monday
1
2
3

Tuesday
1
2
3

Wednesday
1
2
3

Thursday
1
2
3

Friday
1
2
3

Saturday
1
2
3

Sunday
1
2
3

Week of

Monday
1
2
3

Tuesday
1
2
3

Wednesday
1
2
3

Thursday
1
2
3

Friday
1
2
3

Saturday
1
2
3

Sunday
1
2
3

Week of

Monday
1
2
3

Tuesday
1
2
3

Wednesday
1
2
3

Thursday
1
2
3

Friday
1
2
3

Saturday
1
2
3

Sunday
1
2
3

Week of

Monday
1 ___
2 ___
3 ___

Tuesday
1 ___
2 ___
3 ___

Wednesday
1 ___
2 ___
3 ___

Thursday
1 ___
2 ___
3 ___

Friday
1 ___
2 ___
3 ___

Saturday
1 ___
2 ___
3 ___

Sunday
1 ___
2 ___
3 ___

WEEK OF

MONDAY
1
2
3

TUESDAY
1
2
3

WEDNESDAY
1
2
3

THURSDAY
1
2
3

FRIDAY
1
2
3

SATURDAY
1
2
3

SUNDAY
1
2
3

Week of

Monday
1
2
3

Tuesday
1
2
3

Wednesday
1
2
3

Thursday
1
2
3

Friday
1
2
3

Saturday
1
2
3

Sunday
1
2
3

Week of

Monday
1
2
3

Tuesday
1
2
3

Wednesday
1
2
3

Thursday
1
2
3

Friday
1
2
3

Saturday
1
2
3

Sunday
1
2
3

Week of

Monday
1
2
3

Tuesday
1
2
3

Wednesday
1
2
3

Thursday
1
2
3

Friday
1
2
3

Saturday
1
2
3

Sunday
1
2
3

WEEK OF

MONDAY
1
2
3

TUESDAY
1
2
3

WEDNESDAY
1
2
3

THURSDAY
1
2
3

FRIDAY
1
2
3

SATURDAY
1
2
3

SUNDAY
1
2
3

Week of

Monday
1
2
3

Tuesday
1
2
3

Wednesday
1
2
3

Thursday
1
2
3

Friday
1
2
3

Saturday
1
2
3

Sunday
1
2
3

WEEK OF

MONDAY
1
2
3

TUESDAY
1
2
3

WEDNESDAY
1
2
3

THURSDAY
1
2
3

FRIDAY
1
2
3

SATURDAY
1
2
3

SUNDAY
1
2
3

Week of

Monday

1
2
3

Tuesday

1
2
3

Wednesday

1
2
3

Thursday

1
2
3

Friday

1
2
3

Saturday

1
2
3

Sunday

1
2
3

Week of

Monday
1
2
3

Tuesday
1
2
3

Wednesday
1
2
3

Thursday
1
2
3

Friday
1
2
3

Saturday
1
2
3

Sunday
1
2
3

Week of

Monday
1
2
3

Tuesday
1
2
3

Wednesday
1
2
3

Thursday
1
2
3

Friday
1
2
3

Saturday
1
2
3

Sunday
1
2
3

Week of

Monday

1

2

3

Tuesday

1

2

3

Wednesday

1

2

3

Thursday

1

2

3

Friday

1

2

3

Saturday

1

2

3

Sunday

1

2

3

Week of

Monday
1
2
3

Tuesday
1
2
3

Wednesday
1
2
3

Thursday
1
2
3

Friday
1
2
3

Saturday
1
2
3

Sunday
1
2
3

Week of

Monday
1
2
3

Tuesday
1
2
3

Wednesday
1
2
3

Thursday
1
2
3

Friday
1
2
3

Saturday
1
2
3

Sunday
1
2
3

Week of

Monday
1
2
3

Tuesday
1
2
3

Wednesday
1
2
3

Thursday
1
2
3

Friday
1
2
3

Saturday
1
2
3

Sunday
1
2
3

Week of

Monday
1
2
3

Tuesday
1
2
3

Wednesday
1
2
3

Thursday
1
2
3

Friday
1
2
3

Saturday
1
2
3

Sunday
1
2
3

Week of

Monday

1

2

3

Tuesday

1

2

3

Wednesday

1

2

3

Thursday

1

2

3

Friday

1

2

3

Saturday

1

2

3

Sunday

1

2

3

Week of

Monday
1
2
3

Tuesday
1
2
3

Wednesday
1
2
3

Thursday
1
2
3

Friday
1
2
3

Saturday
1
2
3

Sunday
1
2
3

Week of

Monday
1
2
3

Tuesday
1
2
3

Wednesday
1
2
3

Thursday
1
2
3

Friday
1
2
3

Saturday
1
2
3

Sunday
1
2
3

Week of

Monday
1
2
3

Tuesday
1
2
3

Wednesday
1
2
3

Thursday
1
2
3

Friday
1
2
3

Saturday
1
2
3

Sunday
1
2
3

Week of

Monday
1
2
3

Tuesday
1
2
3

Wednesday
1
2
3

Thursday
1
2
3

Friday
1
2
3

Saturday
1
2
3

Sunday
1
2
3

Week of

Monday
1
2
3

Tuesday
1
2
3

Wednesday
1
2
3

Thursday
1
2
3

Friday
1
2
3

Saturday
1
2
3

Sunday
1
2
3

WEEK OF

MONDAY
1
2
3

TUESDAY
1
2
3

WEDNESDAY
1
2
3

THURSDAY
1
2
3

FRIDAY
1
2
3

SATURDAY
1
2
3

SUNDAY
1
2
3

Week of

Monday
1
2
3

Tuesday
1
2
3

Wednesday
1
2
3

Thursday
1
2
3

Friday
1
2
3

Saturday
1
2
3

Sunday
1
2
3

Made in United States
Troutdale, OR
04/13/2025